EVERYDAY MIRACLES

EVERYDAY MIRACLES

Blessings!

Margaret Mayo Gibson, Ed.D.

Margaret Mayo Gibson

Copyright © 2015 by Margaret Mayo Gibson

All rights reserved

AVANTI!

Avanti in Fede Press
Glen Mills, Pennsylvania

ACKNOWLEDGMENTS

I have a heart full of gratitude for all the encouragement and support I received from my family and friends in writing and publishing this book. This is my sixth publication, and it was written despite my low vision. Special thanks to Winnie Hayek for her invaluable help in editing, organizing, and publishing this book.

In giving thanks to my family, I express my deep appreciation for my parents, whose example of love and encouragement continues to be among my life's greatest blessings.

My parents, Margaret and Carl Mayo

Thanks to Lori Gerber who drew the rainbow on the cover of *Everyday Miracles*. Thank you to Susan Smuck for her unfailing devotion to me and my work.

A special thank you to everyone who contributed stories to this book. Without your stories there would be no book!

Note: Some names of authors and of individuals within stories have been changed to protect privacy.

Margaret Mayo Gibson

FOREWORD

"Trust in the Lord with all your heart. Lean not on your own understanding. In all your ways acknowledge Him, and He shall direct your paths" (Proverbs 3:5-6). This verse is my lifelong guide and my inspiration for this book.

Many of the following Everyday Miracles came to me from acquaintances and friends. Other stories here are my own. It is my deep desire that readers recognize the Everyday Miracles in their own lives and share their stories with others.

AVANTI! GO FORWARD!

Margaret Mayo Gibson

CONTENTS

Acceptance Letter	1
All in Jah's Time	4
Blessings of a Warm Fuzzy	8
Bouncing Baby Miracle	13
Close a Door and Open a Window	14
Diamond in the Sand	16
Donna's Story	20
Dream Job	23
Evan Grows Up	26
Father Knows Best	27
Follow Your Dreams!	30
From Vagabond to Therapist	33
Good Old School Days	35
Healing Power of Prayer	36
I Love Miss Schummer!	38
It Was Fated That We Are Mated!	40
Life in Kansas	42
Miracle at Nokosuka	43
Miracle of Life	45
Mother Says!	48
Moving Opens New Doors	51
Musical Miracle	53
Our Little Miracle	55
Out of the Ashes	56
Peggy Becomes a Doctor!	58

Phillies Fans Have to Believe in Miracles	60
Stephen's Story	62
Storytime Friends	66
Taking Advantage of a Second Chance	68
Two Wrongs Make a Right	71
Vindication	74
What Happens When God Intervenes?	77
What's in a Name?	82
With a Little Bit of Luck	84
Looking Ahead	87

ACCEPTANCE LETTER

Ever since I could remember, whenever anyone asked what I wanted to be when I grew up, my response was always the same: a teacher. I come from a long line of educators, and I always felt a sense of joy whenever I was teaching someone. I usually followed up that response with where I wanted to go to college, the University of Delaware.

The campus is beautiful. It's filled with old brick buildings, and it's located in the middle of a town big enough to find everything you need but not so big you feel lost. As I grew up, I had many opportunities to visit the campus—tennis camp each summer, my mom going back to school for her doctorate, and eventually visiting friends as they started their college journey.

I'd had my heart set on going to the University of Delaware since I was a little girl, so when it came time for me to apply to colleges, I knew what my first choice was. I spent hours applying to five or six different colleges, all the while thinking to myself, "Why waste all this time when you already know where you want to end up?"

Weeks went by, and acceptance letters started to come in. I was happy to have all my hard work and achievements recognized by the schools I applied to, but I still hadn't heard from my first choice. One day an envelope finally arrived with the University of Delaware return address. "Woohoo! It's a big envelope so that has to mean good news!" I opened it up and saw the following words:

> Dear Jennifer,
> Congratulations! We are pleased to inform you of your admission to the University of Delaware. Unfortunately, at this time, we cannot admit you into the College of Education, so you will have to start your journey with an undeclared major.

It felt like a pile of bricks had hit me. I had known that the University of Delaware was my number one choice for so long that it never occurred to me that they might not have chosen me back. I tried to be optimistic and look at the positive thing: I had still gotten in. But my dream of becoming a teacher would be delayed until I worked hard enough to show them that I did belong in the education program. I couldn't help but think that there was a chance that might never happen. This was not how this was supposed to turn out. I had everything planned out and organized, and now those plans were changing and things were out of my control.

Over the next few days, I tried to sort through my feelings of disappointment, anger, frustration, and failure. In the end, I decided it might be worth it to visit some of the other schools that I had gotten accepted to. I'd had my heart set on the University of Delaware for so long that I hadn't shown any interest or gotten any information on the other colleges that I had applied to. In the end, my mom convinced me to give it a shot and visit Bloomsburg University.

Everyday Miracles

From the moment I stepped onto Bloomsburg University's campus, I fell in love with it. But this time it wasn't just the beautiful brick buildings or the beautiful campus close to town. I felt a sense of belonging. This was the place I was supposed to be. I went to Bloomsburg for four years and graduated with my education degree. Along the way, I met some of my best friends and made wonderful memories that I will cherish for life.

It was so hard to get the letter from the University of Delaware. At that moment I felt like my dreams had been crushed, but looking back, I can now see how great things turned out.

Graduate Jenny

ALL IN JAH'S[*] TIME

After I graduated from Berklee College of Music, I moved back home and started working at a few part-time jobs. I worked at a burger place in West Chester, Pennsylvania, for the summer. Then in September I subbed for my friend at a gourmet pie, cake, and pastry company for a month while he went on tour with his band. I washed dishes for half the day, then drove all over the place for hours delivering pies and cakes. That ended shortly and I ended up working for my friend's dad in Kennett Square, Pa., at a printing company. Let's just say the best part of the job was driving the van around bringing mail to post offices or bringing the trash to the dump. Fun times!

At this point I had no students to teach drums to and no one really to play/create music with. I was working nine to five every day but only making ten dollars an hour before taxes. Yeah! My dad said the man who worked across the hall from him had a son who played music and needed a drummer. I was desperate to play with anyone, so I agreed to meet with him. He played singer/songwriter/love songs, and I was not really into his music a whole lot. He was solid, a good musician, and we played some fun covers, so I stuck with it for a little while and played a few shows. Let's just say I wasn't that happy with it, and it was not satisfying my musical needs.

A few months later I was still working at the printing company and not really playing with the

---

[*] *Jah* is a shortened form of *Yahweh* (God).

singer/songwriter guy any longer. I hated my job and felt miserable not having a musical group or musical outlet. Something wasn't right, and at that point I realized that if I didn't have some sort of good band or creative expression musically, I was not going to feel fulfilled in any way.

One day I got a call from my friend Micah, who had dropped out of Berklee after two years. When he called me it was probably about two-and-a-half years or more since I had seen him. He was from Delaware and still living at home, but his house wasn't far from mine and was generally in the same area. He said that for the past few months he had been playing in this reggae band in northern Delaware that also played some shows in Philly and other venues in the area. He said they were a solid group and they needed a drummer because he was going to move to Atlanta, Georgia, to join another band. I liked reggae but never played in a reggae band before. I told him to give my number to the band and have them call me. Why not? Let's give it a shot. Why wouldn't I at least meet up with them considering I had nothing with music going on.

A few days later I got a call from the guitar player in the band. He asked, "You went to Berklee, right?" I said, "Yea." He said, "Ok, let's meet up and jam."

A few more days went by and the band came to my house on a Wednesday. We had a great time playing reggae for a few hours. They asked if I would come out to their weekly gig at D & H Jamaican Cuisine the next day to hang out for a set and then maybe play the second set with them. I was hesitant because I didn't know their material at all except for the few hours of jamming, but I said, "Sure."

I showed up at D & H, the restaurant, and it was completely packed. It was their good friend's birthday. They asked me to set up and play all three hours. I was terrified but I set up and did it. They would say a few things before each song and just start playing, and I had no choice but to come up with a beat and play. It went great. I had a great time and everyone loved "the new drummer."

Six-and-a-half years later I still play there every Thursday with a reggae band, Spokey Speaky. We have opened up for some of the biggest reggae acts in the world in some amazing venues in the Philly area over the years and have put on several big shows of our own in Wilmington, Delaware. We still have our residency at D & H every Thursday and a residency every week in the summer in Dewey Beach, De. Also, from playing out in the Delaware music scene all the time with Spokey Speaky, I came into contact with the guys in my funk band, which has been going on for three or more years now!

If Micah hadn't moved and called me up because he knew I was a good drummer in the area and I hadn't taken a chance meeting up with these random guys that played reggae, then none of this would have happened. Maybe I would still be at the printing company. I don't know. I have met some truly amazing people throughout the years playing in Delaware and Philly, made a lot of connections, and have played for some great fans.

Everyday Miracles

The best part of it all is that since joining the group and now still to this day, I am happy with what I'm doing: playing, sharing, creating music, and making a living doing what I love the best in life. Believe in yourself. Do what you love and do it well. If you're feeling bad about the way you're living/making your dough . . . keep going. You never know what might happen.

John Thomas Dickinson

John Thomas Dickinson

THE BLESSINGS OF A WARM FUZZY

In 1991, I was excited to begin my first year of teaching kindergarten in Newburyport, Massachusetts, after four years of long hours studying and student teaching. I'd started college at age thirty-eight and had graduated at age forty-one with a degree in early childhood education and a master's degree in special education.

Before college, I was fortunate to be a stay-at-home mom with our three children and to be earning a little extra for our family by running a small daycare at our home. Children and puppies are two of my favorite things in life! While enjoying those precious growing years with our children, including reading tons of books with them, I came across a book called *T.A. for Tots: And Other Prinzes* (Jalmar Press, 1991), by Alvyn Freed. I was always looking for a positive way to enforce good listening and kind behavior with our own children and the children I nurtured in my private home daycare. The answer came to me in Freed's book when I read about the Warm Fuzzies. The story was illustrated with little, fluffy cotton balls with wings; these Warm Fuzzies bring "feel-good strokes" by being kind to others. The good strokes give warm feelings and make people feel good all over.

Another kind of little creature shares the story with the Warm Fuzzies—the Cold Pricklies. A Cold Prickly looks like a prickly ball with bat wings and a grumpy frown. It gives "bad strokes" that cause shivers up and down the spine, and it does horrid things such as calling people names, hurting their feelings, or making them feel sad or even mad inside. I found my own children and the other children I was taking care of related well to the simple language of the Warm Fuzzy and the Cold Prickly. I decided to bring the concepts into my kindergarten room as gentle, positive behavior management to which my students could easily respond.

During the first three weeks of the school year, I introduced my class to the Warm Fuzzy concept. I asked the children to be a part of my presentation by helping me to tell my story. Some children were drummers or cymbal players who helped me to introduce the Cold Prickly or were bell or triangle players who helped me introduce the Warm Fuzzy. Other children were in the audience and were asked to raise their hands with either a cotton ball for a Warm Fuzzy behavior or a pine cone for a Cold Prickly behavior as the skits demonstrated one or the other.

As we brainstormed, the children helped me list the things the Cold Prickly does: "It bites." "It kicks and pushes." "It doesn't listen." We then decided that the Cold Prickly feels sad and lonely and has no friends. The creature I brought out for everyone to see had a sandpaper belly that, when rubbed, gave chills up and down the spine.

The Warm Fuzzy came out next, and the list of its behaviors grew and grew: "It helps." "It is caring." "It is a good listener." "It hugs you when you feel sad." "It cleans up." There were happy squeals when the children touched the Warm

Everyday Miracles

Fuzzy's lamb's-wool belly. It was unanimous: the Warm Fuzzy feels good inside, is not lonely, and has a lot of friends.

The message was clear to the children. No one wanted to be a Cold Prickly. In fact, the class rule was that after the presentation ended, the Cold Prickly left forever. From then on, no one would ever be called a "Cold Prickly." Someone whose behavior made us think a little of the Cold Prickly might just be having a bad day and have forgotten to bring along the Warm Fuzzies.

All of the children in the twelve kindergarten classes that I would teach were given Warm Fuzzies to remind them of our time together and of the importance of always keeping their Warm Fuzzies with them. The Warm Fuzzy that lived in my classroom was a little handmade, stuffed creature of love that had an embroidered, kind face, just like the ones my mom used to draw on her letters to me. Our class' Warm Fuzzy became famous for comforting child after child who was sad or not feeling well, had scraped a knee, or was having a bad day. Over the years, the Warm Fuzzy was also held and hugged by teachers, principals, and even the superintendent of schools.

The blessings of the Warm Fuzzy came back to me years later. Children who were now in their teens would tell me that they still had their Warm Fuzzy. Some kept it on their bedside table; others hung it on the Christmas tree each year. One Warm Fuzzy was kept in a trophy case; another filled the role of "comforting tool" while its owner was taking the Scholastic Aptitude Test.

I experienced the greatest blessing of the Warm Fuzzy in July 2015, almost thirty-one years after my kindergarteners first met the little creature. My wonderful daughter-in-law, Becky, works as a physical therapist in the Washington, D.C., area. One of her clients—whom I'll call Helen—is a spirited woman in her nineties. Helen took a special liking to my daughter-in-law. When Helen found out that Becky had grown up in Newburyport, Massachusetts, Helen asked her if she knew a Mrs. Gerber. Becky gasped and said, "That's my mother-in-law!"

The story unfolded: Helen's sister, Merry, had a daughter named Penny. Merry had died when Penny was nine, and so Helen had raised Penny. When Penny grew up, she had a son, Darin, and Darin was in one of my kindergarten classes. His mother—Penny—had spoken to me about some of Darin's behavioral concerns, although I don't recall that he ever acted out in class or was a problem for any of the other children.

In August 2015, I received a photograph and a beautiful note that Penny had sent to Helen:

> Mrs. Gerber (Lori), from Brown School, gave Darin this Warm Fuzzy in kindergarten, which changed his life. He has kept it in his room since! He's twenty-six now. She was wonderful to him.

Helen had given the note and photo to my daughter-in-law, who kindly passed them along to me. Receiving the note will remain one of the most touching moments of my life. In reading it, I, too, got that Warm Fuzzy feeling, knowing how much the Warm Fuzzies had meant to Darin.

The legacy of the Warm Fuzzy—which has now been passed along to my seven wonderful grandchildren—will remain one of the precious memories of my life.

Lori Gerber

Darin's Warm Fuzzy

THE BOUNCING BABY MIRACLE

When I was three years old, my mother dressed me in outdoor winter clothing and put me in the back seat of our car. My well-padded winter clothing would later prove useful.

My parents sat up front, and we set out on our way along City Line Avenue, in Philadelphia. This was the era before jump seats for children and even before seat belts. Before we had gone more than a few blocks, I somehow opened the back door of the car as it was traveling thirty-five miles an hour. I fell out onto the road.

Fortunately, the driver following my father had exceptional reflexes and was able to brake in time to avoid running over me. I was taken to the hospital. After a thorough examination, I was released.

My mother described my experience of bouncing out of the car without injury as a miracle. I would have to agree.

John K. Delmar

John K. Delmar

CLOSE A DOOR AND OPEN A WINDOW

Having just finished my master's degree in counseling, I was excited to get into the workforce and use my new knowledge and skills. The market wasn't very open, but I had a friend who had a lead on an opening in her district. I not only was granted an interview but was called back for a follow-up interview and was one of three final candidates. This would be perfect!

I was so disappointed when I didn't get the job and later found out the district had hired internally. It was a long summer hoping for more interviews. Towards the end of the summer I received a call from a district I wasn't familiar with and one to which I hadn't applied. I was a bit confused as to how they got my information. Still being fairly new to the area, I wasn't sure where the district was, but I was happy to go to the interview.

During the interview, I noticed one of the interviewers holding a paper that looked like it had my handwriting on it. I thought I was mistaken, but as I looked closer, it appeared to be a writing sample I had done for that first interview at the other district. I asked where the paper came from and was cleverly averted away from my questioning by being given another question for me to answer.

I was called back for a follow-up interview, and although I thought that was nice, from my past experience I had little hope that it would lead to a job. Going into the second interview, I was thinking of why I wouldn't be disappointed if I didn't get the counseling position. It wasn't ideal as it was a long-term substitute job and I would split between two schools. However, I soon discovered that I was the only candidate called back and this interview was merely a formality for the superintendent to give his approval. I also discovered that the two schools I would be in were each only about ten minutes from where we had land to build our dream house.

I couldn't believe how perfect the job was for me. It was ideal for over the next twenty years. And it wouldn't have come to be if I hadn't gone to that very first interview for which I didn't get the position.

My everyday miracle occurred because an administrator from that first district knew someone from the district who ultimately hired me. My essay and information were sent to my hiring district without my knowledge. Not getting that first position was the best thing that could have happened for my school counseling career!

Karen Dickinson

Karen Dickinson

Everyday Miracles

A DIAMOND IN THE SAND

Our extended family met to celebrate my brother's graduation, a big event for all of us. He was earning a master's degree in education. After the official ceremonies, we set off by ferry for a few days' holiday on Nantucket, an island new to all of us except my brother. He had arranged to rent a large house with outbuildings where all of us could be together. We planned to spend the next day relaxing at the beach and then see my brother off at the small airport so that he could return to work.

We chose a spot on the sand to lay our beach towels close together and then spent a lazy day. We lay in the sun, reapplied sun block, put our toes in the water, and walked a long way beside the water's edge. We enjoyed the snacks and sodas we had brought. While collecting shells and bits of colored glass worn smooth by the sand and waves, I put many of them in the pockets of my shorts and then pulled out handfuls, discarding some. I planned to keep the best ones for craft projects at home.

We realized suddenly that it was time to go if my brother was to make his flight. I made a last visual sweep to make sure we had not left anything behind. From the driver's seat, my brother-in-law was urging me to hurry up. I buckled my seat belt and folded my hands. Then I felt my smooth wedding band, but no diamond was sticking up beside it. With a knot in my stomach I cried out that I had lost my diamond ring!

Immediately my brother-in-law stopped the Jeep. He told me to check my pockets. Saying a quick prayer to St. Anthony, I did just that. However, my pockets held only shells. My brother-in-law said, "If we find it, I'll become a believer."

I thought about how many times I had taken out and replaced shells in my pockets. If the diamond ring had been mixed in with them, it could have fallen into the sand anywhere along my meandering route near the water. Alternately, it could have flipped off my towel as I shook it, if that had been where the ring had been. I never liked to get the diamond gooey with sun lotion or hand cream, so I had a habit of removing the ring when I applied them. Usually I laid it on my lap or right beside me while putting on lotion, but sometimes I would put it in my pocket.

All of us returned to the spot on the beach where we had been, and had a quick but futile search for my diamond. We marked the area with a few sticks and rocks so we could find it again. But then we had to leave or my brother would miss his plane.

Of course I was devastated by my loss, and I continued to pray silently to God while remonstrating with myself for having worn the ring to the beach at all. But there had been no place where we were staying to lock up valuables, so I had worn it. We had recently removed the ring from a separate rider on our home insurance policy to save a little money, and I was reluctant to leave the ring anywhere unsafe.

The next morning, armed with the cooler and rakes found in the garage, my husband and my

Everyday Miracles

brother-in-law went back to the beach to rake the sand in hopes of finding the ring through a methodical search. Starting with the area where the beach towels had been, they raked the top layers of sand, unearthing stones, sticks, shells, and a few bits of plastic, but no ring. They broadened the search area.

Back at the house we busied ourselves with entertaining the children, doing mundane chores, and preparing an evening meal for the group. I prayed through every task that they would find my ring. In tidying up, I came across a local newspaper and a guest book for the house in which we were staying. The book was a place for people to write their thoughts, poems, or essays inspired by their stay there or by events that happened. I started to compose an entry, not for the book but for the lost-and-found section of the local weekly newspaper, in case someone found my ring. However my family advised me to wait, hoping we would find it.

Weary and dirty, the two men returned empty-handed. I spent a quiet evening, feeling miserable and continuing to pray. My husband, David, was understandably as upset as I was about the loss.

The following morning, the men again left for the beach, this time along with our teenage son. In between praying, I resolved to keep busy and do whatever I could to recover the ring. I rewrote the lost-and-found notice, getting it ready to submit to the newspaper, and made a few "lost" posters to put on the fence at the beach. Then to distract myself, I started reading the guest book. Some entries were about the weather, beautiful sunsets, or the ocean.

Everyday Miracles

Other entries told about interesting things that had happened. One entry in particular caught my attention, so I showed it to my mother and sister. Someone had come a few years earlier with children and grandchildren and spent a day on the beach playing in the sand. The next words were, "Lost and found my diamond ring, a real miracle." I could scarcely believe it! I prayed with renewed effort.

About midafternoon, the searchers returned looking dejected and put the rakes away for the night. I showed them the lost-and-found notice and suggested we take it to the newspaper office on our way to dinner. They pooh-poohed my efforts, but I thought it was important. What if someone found the ring after we left the island?

The men got cleaned up for going out. I sat downheartedly on the bed. "Time to go!" the others called. I said to go without me; I wasn't hungry anyway. My son was sent back up to get me. I told him I didn't want to go; I was too miserable. My son said nothing, but then he slowly brought one hand up where I could see that he was wearing my ring! The diamond's shine was undiminished except for a black speck on one side of it. My son had realized that he and the men couldn't make me wait until dinner to learn about the miracle.

Needless to say, since then my diamond ring spends most of its time in our safety deposit box at the bank—and never goes to the beach. Before leaving I made an entry in the guest book referring back to the date of the earlier diamond ring miracle. Imagine a second diamond ring being lost and found in the sand: a second miracle!   Diane Scott

DONNA'S STORY

I was asked to write about something that turned out just right after an uncertain start.

As I pondered the topic, my thoughts took me back to my teen years when I wondered about many things: Which college would I attend, what would be my career choice, would I ever marry and have a husband and kids? Would there be a home with a white picket fence in the future for me?

Idyllic thoughts for the most part . . . until the somewhat scary realization that a husband and an "I do" would likely include a mother-in-law too. This unknown was a bit frightening.

What would she be like? Would she wear white gloves for dust detection during visits to our home? Housekeeping was not my strength. How would I measure up to the expectations that she might hold for the wife of her son?

Now after thirty-four years of marriage and an equal number of years in a mother-in-law relationship, let me share some experiences that followed that prenuptial period of anxious anticipation and fear.

Mom did come to visit. Thankfully she left the white gloves at home and never once seemed to comment on the dirty floors and windows or less-than-tidy bedrooms.

Although her home was in tiptop order, she did not seem to be bothered that our abode did not enjoy the same degree of organization. There were no negative comments or criticisms from Mom, but instead a cheerful demeanor of tolerance.

It was Mom's tradition to make a blueberry pie for my husband's birthday celebration. I remember the day I came home from the hospital with our first-born son. There on the table was Mom's freshly baked blueberry birthday pie, the best pie I have ever eaten. It was a delightful treat after two days of hospital food.

Mom shared the blueberry pie recipe with me years ago. However to date, I have never made a blueberry pie. I buy pies for my husband at the local fruit stand. They are good but not as delicious as Mom's fresh out-of-the-oven masterpiece. Yet there has been no recommendation for celebratory desserts at our birthday parties. Instead, Mom displays a genuine kind of gratefulness and joyfulness at family gatherings, no matter the menu.

I recall struggling with an overwhelming workload at my new job. It was clear to me that I needed to pick up the pace. However it was clear to my mother-in-law that the pace was unjustified and inappropriate. Years later when I look back on that work situation and other hard times, I think to myself how wonderful it was to always have my mother-in-law in my corner providing an ongoing voice of positive support. Just as important were all the instances when she kept silent instead of offering guidance and advice. No matter the situation, I always felt like she was on my side.

You get the drift: I was treated like one of her own. Life is good. I married a loving, gentle, and kind man, created from the same mold as his mother. Despite the odds, I ended up being the winner in the Family Jackpot. I am one of the lucky ones.

Donna Gibson

Donna and Margaret (who considers *herself* the lucky one)

DREAM JOB

Graduating from college can be one of the most exciting and nerve-racking times in someone's life. I know in the weeks leading up to graduation I was filled with an excitement over achieving my goals and marking off a milestone in my life by earning a college degree. Along with this came a sense of responsibility to start a career and become successful, so it was important to me that I started off on the right foot.

For two summers during my college career, I interned for a company that opened my eyes to the possibilities of what I could be doing after graduation. It made me excited about the major that I chose and how well the education I was getting fit the expectations of this company. After completing my second internship between my junior and senior years of college, I was almost certain that I would be a shoo-in after graduation and would seamlessly just move into a full-time position at this company.

It came time to submit applications for full-time positions because we would soon be graduating, so I applied for a position at the company. After a few weeks of waiting, I was given the news that I was not awarded the job that I thought I would get so easily. The other candidate had been given the job, and I was crushed by this news.

I quickly scrambled to find another job, and just before graduation I got a job at a company over an hour away from where I was living at my parents' house. I had no choice but to take it because I needed the experience and the money, and this was my only chance at that moment. I can't say that my experience at this different company was all bad because it allowed me to see a different side of the manufacturing world that I was never exposed to. After two months of driving through summer shore traffic to get to work, I was beginning to think I would either need to find a different job or move closer to work so I didn't have to deal with the stressful commute.

One random day during that summer of 2006, I received a call from the original company where I had tried so hard to get a job. They were looking to fill a full-time position, and they wanted me to come in and interview. Long story short, I was awarded the full-time position and could finally breathe a sigh of relief.

At the time, receiving the news that I didn't get the job made me scramble. I wondered what would happen to me because I had envisioned myself at this company for so long I couldn't see past that. In hindsight, it made me appreciate my job that much more, and I am grateful that I was given the opportunity to be able to see things that way. I am still working at this same company and couldn't be happier with how things turned out.

Jeff Lane

Jeff Lane

EVAN GROWS UP

When my grandson Evan was sixteen months old, he was diagnosed with Wilms Tumor, a form of cancer. The family was devastated. What followed was a series of surgeries, including the removal of one kidney, chemotherapy treatment, and radiation. Evan's mother, Rhonda, my daughter, stayed in the hospital with him, going home only to get fresh clothes.

Evan was in Alfred I. duPont Hospital for Children. He got the best care from the doctors and nurses. It was sad to see some children in the halls one day, then never see them again.

Through it all, Evan remained cooperative and uncomplaining. This remarkable young man is now seventeen years old and will graduate from high school next year!

Barbara McFadden

Evan

FATHER KNOWS BEST

I was sixteen and getting ready for my high school graduation exercises when a neighbor came to the door to return a tool he had borrowed from Carl, my dad. "Congratulations!" he said to me. "Good luck in finding a full-time job."

My dad heard that and said, "No, Joe, Peggy is going to college so she will not be looking for a full-time job for a while."

"College!" Joe replied. "What a waste! She's a girl! She will get married and have kids. You don't need a college education to have a baby!"

Carl responded, "She is going to college. Thanks for returning the tool." Dad quietly closed the front door. I was fortunate that my father did not hold the view prevalent at that time—the 1940's—that girls were to stay home, clean house, and raise children.

When I heard I had an opportunity to attend college, I was ecstatic! No one in my neighborhood or in my high school circle of friends was able to do that. My parents told me that I could enroll right after graduation. My joy turned to frustration, however, when I learned that I had no choice of colleges. I dreamed of a garden campus and living in a dorm. The reality was that since my father worked at Temple Hospital full time, I could attend Temple University tuition free. It was the only way my family could afford to send me to college.

When I protested, my father said, "Go to Temple or go to work." I decided to go to work. I had no idea where I could work. I was sixteen years old and was graduating from an academic high school with no typing skills. Dad said he got me a job at Temple University.

The day after my high school graduation in January 1948, I started working. I commuted to Temple each day taking a trolley, subway, and bus. My job was to deliver handouts to several classes. The professors had left the master copies to be run off the day before. Each time I entered a classroom I looked at the chalkboards. How interesting, I thought! I looked forward to studying the bulletin boards. After three weeks I decided to attend Temple! My mother reminded me that since the semester had started I would have to wait until fall to enroll. "By then you will really appreciate the opportunity Dad is giving you," Mom said. "In the meantime, you must keep your job and not be idle. That would be an insult to God!"

In the fall I continued commuting to Temple, this time as a student. I received a great education, made lifelong friends, and in my junior year met the man who would become my husband!

Margaret Mayo Gibson

Dad at work at Temple U.

Everyday Miracles

A happy graduation day

My handsome dad

FOLLOW YOUR DREAMS!

When I was a child I heard stories from my mother's mother, Grandmom Giovanna, about Italy, especially the village of Montaguto, east of Naples, where she was born. I was fascinated with the details of life in Montaguto. I dreamed of visiting there someday.

Many years passed and though my parents and grandparents were gone, I still had my dream. When I approached seventy my husband and children said they wanted me to take a "roots" trip to visit Montaguto. Since both my mother's parents and my father's parents were all born in Montaguto, I was thrilled at the prospect.

Finding Montaguto was not easy. It was not on any map I had. When I called the embassy in Washington, I was told the village never existed. I made several calls with the same results. Although my grandparents were not formally educated, I was sure they knew the name of the village where they were born! When I expressed that to one embassy official, he said, "Then it must have been destroyed in an earthquake because it does not exist today."

Weeks passed and I was trying to cope with my disappointment. Then one day my husband, Tom, and I were in Borders bookstore, each of us perusing different subjects. Suddenly, Tom called to me. "Honey, come here. Is this what you have been looking for?" My husband was pointing to a spot on a map of Italy which said "Montaguto"!

We had arrived in Montaguto and had found a cousin, hotel, and guide. Then, on the last day of our visit, we were on the beach in Gallipoli when we heard a big commotion. People were shouting, but neither of us could understand a word until I heard someone scream, "ACCIDENTE!" I said to Tom, "There has been a terrible accident somewhere!"

We had continued our walk just a few steps when we heard someone scream, "NO ACCIDENTE! TERRORISTA!" I thought that sounded like terrorists had struck somewhere! Tom suggested we return to the hotel and watch a TV news channel in English. We did. What we saw and heard was devastating! It was September 11, 2001. We were due to come home the next day but our flight was cancelled. For the next three days, I prayed hard ... for Tom and me to live to see our family again! On the fourth day after 9/11, we got a flight and returned home safely, thank God.

Margaret Mayo Gibson

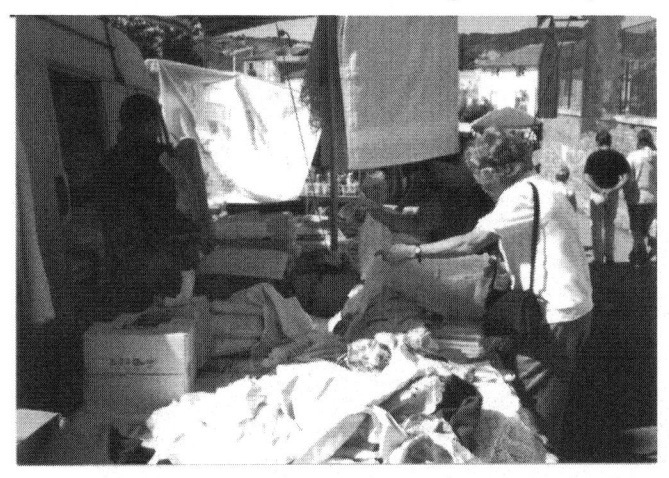

Shopping for lace in Montaguto

Everyday Miracles

Margaret (Margie) looking at the Bay of Naples

FROM VAGABOND TO THERAPIST

When my high-school girlfriend married, I could no longer afford to rent the apartment we had shared on the edge of the California desert. I chose to go east to where I had never been before.

I packed up all my meager belongings and took the Greyhound bus, riding for three days and nights to Pittsburgh. I chose Pittsburgh because a former classmate lived there. I thought she might be able to suggest where to apply for employment and find a safe place to live. She lived in a residence for single women. However, she was very much a loner and was not helpful.

Getting a job was imperative for me. I looked for the Bureau of Rehabilitation Services, a state agency that assists the handicapped, because I have only one eye. I could not find that office, so I contacted the Council for the Blind. This agency felt that I might qualify for their services and asked me to come to their office for an interview.

The agent there sent me to be tested. The tests showed that I was qualified for college, so the agent assisted me in filling out an application for the University of Pittsburgh and in applying for a chancellor's scholarship. He also sent me to an eye and ear hospital for a job interview.

I became a cleaning lady in the hospital. The head housekeeper learned of my story and was most helpful. She knew that I would have times when I needed to go to the university for class-placement testing. She arranged to have two high-school girls, who were working in the hospital for the summer, keep the cleaning going for me while I was at the university for my testing.

By a series of miracles, I got into college and got through the first three years. When it came time to apply for physical-therapy school, the housekeeper, one of the doctors I sometimes worked with after I became a nurse's aide, and my German-language professor wrote recommendations for me.

I did get my degree in physical therapy. Thank the Lord!

What looked like a lost cause became a very fruitful adventure.

Delilah Foldes

Delilah Foldes

THE GOOD OLD SCHOOL DAYS

I wondered why I had to change schools now, to start sixth grade. I was doing well in my subjects, had many friends, and had never been in trouble. It was because my mother was protesting a transportation policy recently implemented by the public school system.

She decided to put me in Catholic school. I cried the whole night before I was to start. I went off to Catholic school feeling very sad. But what happened then let me experience the good old school days!

The priest and the nuns were very kind to me. My parents were both doctors. My mother treated the nuns for free when they were ill, so the Catholic school waived my tuition. The curriculum was far advanced from the public school I had left, which made Catholic school much more appealing and motivated me to enjoy school. Also, there was Philip, a boy who had been in all my classes and whose parents sent him to the same Catholic school when I went. It was comforting to know someone really understood what I was going through. With kind nuns and kind priests, an interesting curriculum, and Philip, it seemed like a miracle that a forced school transition I had feared became a wonderful change in my life! Mary Smith

Mary and Chauncey Smith

THE HEALING POWER OF PRAYER

One evening in July 1976, we were on our way to Lewis, Delaware, when a car ran into us, hitting my side of the car. We were not wearing seat belts and my leg was crushed. I ended up at Wilmington Hospital, where a surgeon made a twelve-inch incision in my leg and placed an eighteen-inch steel rod through my hip into my leg. The pain was so intense that I screamed every time I moved.

After nine months, my leg still had not healed. The surgeon suggested another operation; I did not like the idea. A girl who worked in the store that we owned asked if I knew of charismatic healing. I had never heard of it, but I was willing to find out, though some family and friends were opposed.

I followed my inner voice and attended a meeting. I saw a huge crowd of people shouting praises to God in hope for healing and decided that if that many believed, then I could too! That week I went to church, set my eyes on the cross, and prayed: "God if you really do perform real miracles on real people, please heal my leg."

The congregation began the Lord's Prayer. When we came to the part, "Forgive our trespasses as we forgive those who trespass against us," I heard a voice say to me, "You are asking me to forgive you, but you have not forgiven the man who hit you." I cried, "Oh, my God, I forgive him. I will drop all charges against him." I could not believe that God had actually spoken to me!

Everyday Miracles

During the mass we heard that a lady's fractured leg was being healed. My friend grabbed my leg and I screamed in pain, but she would not let go. When she finally did, the pain was gone. I kept touching my leg, but there was no pain. I knew then that I was healed.

On my next visit to the surgeon, he said he was considering another operation but of course would take extensive x-rays first, which he did. When we met to discuss the x-rays, he asked me what had happened. I told him about charismatic healing, and he advised me to continue meetings now to heal my knee, which was also a problem.

Mariann Venuti

Sam and Mariann Venuti
on their twenty-fifth anniversary

I LOVE MISS SCHUMMER!

I liked first grade except for math. I just did not understand the concepts! I did very well in every other subject. I began erasing my wrong math answers so often that I was tearing holes in my math papers. My teacher, Miss Schummer, told me to stop erasing so hard, but I could not stop.

One day, Miss Schummer took all of my pencils and cut off all the erasers. I went home crying and devastated. My mother had been telling me to "just do your best." I insisted that I already was but it was doing no good. I continued crying.

Finally, my mother asked for a conference with Miss Schummer and told her how upset I was. The next day math class was different! I found Miss Schummer to be patient and compassionate! I responded well to my teacher's new attitude and ended up with a B in math! To this day, I still hate math, but I still love Miss Schummer.

Lori Gerber

Everyday Miracles

Miss Schummer's first-grade class
(Lori Gerber is the girl with a heart on her picture.)

Everyday Miracles

IT WAS FATED THAT WE ARE MATED!

When I was a college freshman at Temple University, I met Gary. We had dated regularly for over a year. Gary was now a senior and told me he wanted to get engaged after he graduated. I was thrilled! One month later Gary called me. A new student had transferred into Gary's department and he had fallen in love with her! I was understandably shocked as I said goodbye to Gary.

Just three weeks later, I got a phone call. An unfamiliar voice said that he was a senior at Temple, had seen me around campus, and wanted to date me. He was graduating in three weeks and wanted to take me to a picnic on campus. On April 28, 1951, Tom Gibson and I had our first date. We were mutually attracted to each other and quickly realized that we were compatible. Tom graduated and got a job. We continued to date.

Two months later I got a call from Gary. He said that he had made a big mistake and realized that I was the one he really cared for. I told him about Tom. The next week I got a call from a friend of Gary's telling me that Gary really meant it when he said he wanted us to get back together. I explained that Tom was the only one I was interested in dating. I never saw Gary again. I thank God that Tom and I have been married sixty-two years and Tom is still the love of my life!

Margaret Mayo Gibson

Everyday Miracles

Tom and Margie, April 11, 1953, in Philadelphia

Everyday Miracles

LIFE IN KANSAS

I grew up in Kansas in the thirties. Summer in Kansas was hot. Western Kansas was in the Dust Bowl. Eastern Kansas, where I lived, had dust in the air and on window sills. My mother wiped the window sills every morning; I washed the dust out of my ears every night when I bathed.

I played with the boys in the neighborhood because I liked what they played—baseball and football. I especially liked football, and I was a pretty good player.

My mother made me quit playing tackle football when I was fourteen. I was going to high school and other activities attracted me. I still played sports, but it was with girls—and it wasn't football.

I didn't date much in high school because I had played football with most of the boys in my class. I was attracted to Earl in my senior year. When my sister and I walked to town, I made her walk on the sunny side of the street because I might see Earl working in his father's service station.

On graduation night, a friend who lived in the country was having a party. I asked Earl if I could ride with him in his Model A. The party became a date.

We were married when we both finished college. Clint graduated on June 5 and had a bachelor party on June 6; we were married on June 7. We have four children, eight grandchildren, and seven greats. We have been married for sixty-five years and are still happy.   **Hortense McDuffee**

MIRACLE AT NOKOSUKA

When I was approaching eighteen, World War II was raging, and I enlisted in the U.S. Navy in February of my senior year of high school. Since I left before the end of the year, I missed covering electricity in science class.

By the time basic training was completed, the war had ended, and I was sent to Pearl Harbor, where I was given a two-week course on the rewinding and splicing of film and the operation of sixteen-millimeter movie projectors. I wanted to learn more, so I signed out a book from the Pearl Harbor Navy Library on radio repair.

Next, I was flown to Japan, ending up at the Fleet Motion Picture Exchange in Yokosuka, where I spent day after day rewinding film. In my spare time, I studied the book on radio repair (which I'd brought along with me). I could see from my reading that the amplifiers in movie projectors had much in common with those of radios. Because of this, I arranged to work the second shift of film rewinding so I could spend time in the sound shop, where electronic-technician petty officers were repairing movie sound systems.

Not long after this, both petty-officer technicians were discharged from the Navy, leaving no one in charge of repairing the systems. I was given a chance to do it!

Shortly after taking over this job, the sound system in the Enlisted Men's Club failed. Those projectors were full-sized thirty-five-millimeter

Everyday Miracles

projectors, such as are used in movie theaters. I was called in to check and repair the defective system. When I arrived there I was shocked to find both a pre-amplifier and a full amplifier on each projector, something totally unknown to me. Not knowing what else to do, I pulled out the Simpson Ohmmeter I'd brought along and measured one of the many resisters on the amplifier. Lo and behold, it was bad! Miraculously, I had chosen the one out of hundreds of possible defective resistors, capacitors, and inductors that could have malfunctioned! I replaced it, and the projector worked flawlessly.

After this, I was known as the go-to person for repairs!

Ernest H. Bogert

Ernest Bogert (l) with a friend
in Yokosuka, Japan, February 1946

THE MIRACLE OF LIFE

As a volunteer EMT in the community of Oakhurst, New Jersey, I learned a lot about life. I was there at the end of life more times than I care to remember. But the miracle and mystery of the beginning of life are what fascinate me. The beginning of life shows how God views a child as special.

One night, about eleven o'clock, my emergency pager went off. The dispatcher said a baby had been tossed into a garbage dumpster. I had to take a moment to comprehend what he'd said because I couldn't believe my ears. I got out of bed, threw on some clothes, and raced to the scene as fast as I could.

When I got to the scene, I found that a volunteer fireman was very near and had heard the call. He pulled in and got the baby out of the dumpster. When I got there I found the fireman sitting in the back of the police car. Due to my large size, I couldn't get in with him. I opened the door of the car and he said the baby was doing fine. Because it was a cold night, I closed the door of the police car to keep them warm.

The ambulance and paramedics arrived quickly and rendered the best possible care. Then it occurred to me, we have another patient! I asked the police officer to come with me, and we followed the trail of blood right to the apartment door of the mother. I knocked on the door as hard as I could. The mother opened the door and sat down on the

Everyday Miracles

chair. I asked her if she had just had a baby. She nodded yes.

The police officer radioed for another ambulance while I rendered emergency care to the teenage mother. The second ambulance arrived fast and we were preparing to bring the mother downstairs when the grandmother came home. The police officer told her what had happened and the grandmother collapsed in the chair repeating, "Oh my God!"

We brought the mother downstairs on a stair chair and then transferred her to the stretcher. One of the female EMTs who was in the ambulance said she didn't think she could take care of the mother after what she had done. I offered to take her place in the ambulance, but I reminded her that EMTs don't have the luxury of showing emotions until after the call is finished. She changed her mind and rode with the mother to the hospital. After the ambulances and paramedics left, I went back home too wired up to sleep.

The timeline of the emergency went like this: The mother got pregnant and hid the pregnancy due to her weight. The mother gave birth in a bathtub full of water. The mother put the baby in a garbage bag and took it to the dumpster, leaving a trail of blood. By some miracle, the baby cleared his airway enough to cry. Someone came home from work and heard the baby crying inside the dumpster and called the police. The rest you know.

There were many miracles happening here. It was a miracle the baby survived the ordeal. It was a miracle that someone cared enough to get involved and call the police. It was a miracle a fireman was close by and pulled the baby from the dumpster. It was also a miracle that the fireman was a father and knew how to take care of the baby. It was a miracle that a trail of blood was left so we could trace it back to the mother and give her emergency care. God worked overtime that night.

Carl Mayo

Margaret Gibson with Michelle and Carl Mayo

MOTHER SAYS!

My mother's parents, Giovanna and Vincenzo Borrelli, were immigrants from southern Italy. They came to America as newlyweds with their passage paid by a factory in Winsted, Connecticut. When the factory closed, they found work as migrant farmers. When my mother was born, she went with her parents to plant and harvest. She, like her parents, never had any schooling at all. From the time she was a teenager through her adulthood, my mother worked in a sewing factory. Though she never even went to first grade, she worked all year, twelve hours a day, to send my dad through college.

One day I came home from school very frustrated. I said to my mother, "All the girls in my class keep talking about their dolls and bikes. I don't have either one." My mother replied, "What is your last name?" I said, "Mom, you know my last name. It is the same as yours!" Mom said, "Say it." I replied, "Mayo." Mom said, "In the Mayo house we do not need dolls and bikes. Go outside and play running tag; it is healthier." So I did.

My third-grade teacher was absent one day and the substitute kept saying, "You poor, poor kids, living in South Philadelphia!" When I got home, I said to my mom, "I didn't know we were poor!" Mom said, "We are not poor. Who said we are poor?" I told my Mom what the substitute teacher had said. Mom replied, "We are not poor because you have food, clothing, and shelter; God loves you,

you have a family who loves you, and you have lots of friends. You are not poor. Now go out and play."

I said, "I know: play tag!"

"Right!" said Mom.

I was hungry and wondered when dinner would be ready. "In a minute," said Mom. "What are we having?" I asked. "Beans and rice," Mom said. "Mom, we had that last night!" I relied. "No, last night we had rice and beans! Sit down and eat. It is good for you."

"I do not want to keep visiting Aunt Edith. She is so grouchy," I told my mom. My mom replied that Edith had no family and she was lonely. "Besides, when you get old," said Mom, "people will then be nice to you."

"Promise?"

"Yes!" said Mom.

I did not understand how my mother could make such a promise, but she would not change her mind, so I continued to make the visits. I am so glad I did. Now that I am old, people are really nice to me, so I guess Mom was right!

After visiting a friend one day, my mother said she needed to talk with me. She said, "I went to visit my dear friend Eleanor today. Her niece Cathy was there. Every time Eleanor started to speak, Cathy interrupted her and told her she was using poor grammar. Eleanor was embarrassed. Don't correct your elders. Remember, good manners are better than good English!"

My mother never went to school, but as my dad always said, she was one of the smartest people I have ever known.   Margaret Mayo Gibson

Everyday Miracles

Welcome sign for Winsted, Connecticut,
my mother's birthplace

My mother, Margaret Mayo

MOVING OPENS NEW DOORS

I didn't really want to move across the river to a different state. It wasn't very far, but I liked our home and our friends, and we would be moving farther from our families. It was not a great time to move; I was expecting our second child in a few months. However, my husband's new job was in the new state and his commute had been horrific. I wasn't working as I was staying home to raise our children, so I had no reason not to move.

Before I stopped working I was thinking about going back to school for my master's degree. I enjoyed teaching and wanted to stay in the school system; however, I wanted to do something to help the students who were more at risk. I had looked into the programs around where we lived, and although nothing fit exactly with what I wanted, I thought a master's degree in social work was the closest program which matched my desires. I would have to look for programs in our new locale.

A year after our move and the birth of our second child, I got a catalog for the closest college to our home. I was ready to start taking courses, and I read through the social work section of the catalog. The courses sounded okay, just not what I had in mind. I still wanted to have direct contact with students in school and be a support to them and their parents and the school staff. I started to put the catalog down when I happened to notice a page on school counseling. My high school counselor had

Everyday Miracles

been no help to me, so I had never considered school counseling, but perhaps it couldn't hurt to look.

Wait, what was this in the catalog? An elementary-school counseling program? I had never heard of an elementary-school counselor. There were no elementary-school counselors in the state where I had taught, and that was right across the river. As I read through the coursework descriptions, it was as though they had made the program just for me. I couldn't believe it! If we had not moved, I would never have found the perfect master's program for me and the start of a wonderful career.

Karen Dickinson

Graduate Karen with her proud parents,
Tom and Margie Gibson

A MUSICAL MIRACLE

In my fifth month of being stationed in Korea, I was reading the military newspaper *Pacific Stars and Stripes* when I saw an article that captured my attention. The article was asking for an officer who knew music and could head up a show to substitute for Bob Hope's show. At that time, Bob Hope was only doing his shows every other year, and this was to be his off year.

I went to division headquarters to audition. They immediately offered me the position and placed orders that removed me from my rifle company position. I became the "officer in charge" of eighteen soldiers who were very talented. Because of our combined abilities, I was able to form a men's glee club. Within this group I created a vocal quartet, a jazz combo, and a Spanish singing trio. We also featured comedy skits and a good master of ceremonies. In addition to being the officer in charge and directing the glee club, I played trumpet in the jazz combo and sang in the vocal quartet.

Soldiers far away from home loved to be entertained. We were booked to perform all over South Korea and became renowned. Sometimes we had over two thousand in the audience, soldiers who were trucked in from their outposts for the entertainment. We were also given a Sunday-night TV show on the Armed Forces Korean Network. This half-hour show was televised live in the studios of Seoul.

Everyday Miracles

    The U.S. Fifth Air Force was stationed in Japan, and their commanding officer viewed one of our shows. He went through his chain of command all the way up to the Pentagon and back down to my army division and was able to get military orders for my group to tour and entertain our troops in Japan. What an experience!

John K. Delmar

John K. Delmar

OUR LITTLE MIRACLE

It was a lovely spring day, and our six-year-old son, Rick, was playing baseball with the neighborhood children in front of our home. Suddenly he ran into the house wheezing and coughing up blood. Immediately I put him into the car and rushed him to the doctor. The bleeding subsided, but the doctor insisted on sending him to Children's Hospital of Philadelphia. He was kept there overnight for observation and some tests. Since they found nothing wrong, he was released and sent home.

Exactly one week later, the incident occurred again in the middle of the night. We rushed him back to CHOP, where they did extensive testing for an entire week while I stayed by his side day and night. Again, they found no cause for the bleeding and found nothing at all wrong with Rick.

Rick is now forty-five years old, married with a family of his own, and has never had a recurrence of this incident.

I attribute this miracle to the many prayers of our family, friends, and his second-grade classmates.

Joan Ann Mayo

Rick Mayo with his parents, Bob and Joan

OUT OF THE ASHES

What would you do if your childhood home burned to the ground and the only evidence of the first twenty years of your life was a list of items to be submitted to an insurance company? What do you think it would feel like to see all of those years on a spreadsheet?

When I went through my own list and took inventory of my childhood, I was surprised by what I found. For one thing, I couldn't believe how much money I had spent on baseball cards. But as sad as it was to lose those cards (and toys, books, clothes, and knick-knacks) it also gave me an opportunity to reflect on why those objects had meaning in the first place. To be sure, most of them had very little monetary value, and I had long ago given up hope that my Beanie Baby collection would be the key to an early retirement.

Instead, I held onto those childhood mementos because they helped me make sense of the world and find my place in it. By going through the exercise of creating the list of objects and sharing it with friends and family, I was not only able to relive good times from long ago but I also gained a perspective on how I became the person I am today.

Brad Gibson

Everyday Miracles

Brad Gibson

PEGGY[†] BECOMES A DOCTOR!

I finished college and became a teacher. I married, had two children, and stayed home to care for them until my younger child was eight years old. I returned to teaching. One day the principal assigned a student teacher to me and admired my mentoring ability so much that he assigned me student teachers permanently! I became passionate about my mentoring role and decided to earn a doctorate to teach aspiring teachers. I was in my fifties and decided not to wait any longer.

It would not be easy to pay the necessary tuition! My husband's company, for which he had worked twenty-eight years, had just decided to move to Texas. He did not want to move, and he did not have a prospect of a job! Our son was in medical school and our daughter was in college.

Considering all the financial circumstances, the only way for me to get the doctorate was to be an adjunct instructor and have my tuition paid. The dean said that was impossible because there were hundreds of eligible people ahead of me. I persisted. The dean said, "Why? Didn't you hear me? There are hundreds ahead of you on the list!" I pleaded to be put on the list. He finally agreed.

Two weeks later I got a phone call telling me to appear for an interview that day! I needed to know what had happened to that list! The dean said that

---

[†] Margaret Mayo Gibson's family and childhood friends know her as "Peggy." More recent acquaintances know her as "Margie."

the professor who was eligible for an adjunct could not keep an adjunct more than two weeks but that I, being mature (older), would last longer!

I got the job and soon discovered why others had lasted only two weeks. The professor spent her time doing research for promotion while the adjunct did the planning, teaching, and evaluating. The professor collected her full salary all along! After three years I received a doctorate and a world of experience with a great recommendation from the professor, which led to a position on the faculty.

Margaret Mayo Gibson

Mama's proud!

PHILLIES FANS HAVE TO BELIEVE IN MIRACLES

Over the past 132 years, the Philadelphia Phillies have lost 10,650 games. No team in recorded history has lost more. So it is not a stretch to say that on the evening of October 27, 2008, the fact that the Phillies had a chance to win just their second World Series was a miracle. Unfortunately, millions of other Phillies fans in the Delaware Valley area agreed, making tickets exceedingly expensive and difficult to procure.

That afternoon, I scoured the Internet until I stumbled upon a pair of tickets, which I immediately purchased. Moments later, I received a call informing me that the tickets I had just bought had already been purchased by someone else. But I wouldn't take no for an answer, and somehow, after a rendezvous in a shady Holiday Inn backroom, I had two tickets to the game.

The Phillies got out to an early lead and were just ten outs away from the finish line. And then the rain started. . . .

As I watched the grounds crew pull the tarp over the soaked infield just after the Phillies surrendered their lead, doubt crept in. Perhaps I had made a terrible mistake investing so heavily in this game. In fact, there was a great deal of evidence in the history of this team to suggest that such an investment was, at best, criminally insane.

But, eventually, the rain did stop. The Phillies took the field again two days later to resume the game and quickly regained the lead. Of course, they promptly lost it again and reduced me to a puddle of panicked mumblings before finally taking the lead for good and closing out the series.

While I haven't been around for all 10,650 of the Phillies' losses, I've certainly seen my fair share. But past failures, a couple thousand dollars, and four inches of rain are not good enough reasons to deny the possibility of a happy ending. It might take another 132 years, but I'll be ready when the next one comes around.

Gregory Gibson

Gregory Gibson

STEPHEN'S STORY

My son, Stephen Pague, was born on Friday, January 5, 1990, at about four o'clock in the afternoon. He was a beautiful, healthy-looking redhead, and the delivery had brought no concerns. Stephen's dad, Jeff, and I were exhausted but thrilled. That evening, Stephen's grandmother and great-grandmother both mentioned that he seemed to be spitting up quite a bit, but I—a nurse—felt that everything was normal.

About 5 a.m. the next morning, a neonatologist whom I had not met before woke me to tell me that our baby was going to be transferred to St. Christopher's Hospital for Children, in Philadelphia. Stephen's oxygen level was declining, and he was not able to keep down fluids. Because of my low hemoglobin level, my doctor would not release me to accompany Stephen, who by now was receiving an IV and oxygen. I asked my nurse to bring me some water. I poured a little of the water over the top of my baby's head and baptized him in the name of the Father, the Son, and the Holy Spirit. Jeff followed the ambulance downtown from our suburban hospital; I was inconsolable, overwhelmed with worry.

After many tests and procedures, Stephen's doctors determined that he had a connection between his esophagus and his trachea (called a *tracheal esophageal fistula*) and that fluids were going into his lungs. One result was a mild pneumonia. One of Stephen's doctors called me and explained that Stephen's condition is often associated with multiple kidney, heart, and spine issues. I was frantic and wanted the corrective surgery performed as soon as possible.

When Stephen was five days old, a priest arrived and baptized him officially. Stephen was then taken into surgery. The surgery lasted at least two hours longer than the anticipated four hours because our baby's condition was even more complex than his doctors had anticipated. We weren't able to hold our little boy for three days, which just about killed us. It took more than two weeks for him to heal so that the leaking between his esophagus and trachea completely stopped.

After weeks of taking no nourishment by mouth, Stephen had lost the newborn sucking reflex. It was torture to reteach him how to suck the nipple, and for days he would only swallow a couple of tablespoonsful at a time. Finally, on January 29, we brought our baby home.

But just over a month after that, the doctors discovered that Stephen had another fistula. Again, all nourishment by mouth had to cease. On March 19, Stephen was back in surgery, and again the surgery was longer and more complex than anticipated.

The doctors were pleased by the outcome, but when we first saw our baby in the ICU after the surgery, we were overcome by emotion to see our little rosy-faced son looking shockingly pale. Yet when he came to, we were comforted by his healthy cry. That night brought another scare, but the

Everyday Miracles

problem proved to be mucus and was quickly resolved.

Even then, healing did not go smoothly. What was first a small leak at the surgery site was larger a week later. Stephen was readmitted to the hospital. But this time, surgery was not needed. We brought our baby back home, and healing finally began in earnest. Toward the end of April, Stephen was taking all of his nutrition by mouth, and two weeks later, his feeding tube was removed. A week after that, our four-and-a-half-month-old baby was in the car with us on the way to Nags Head, North Carolina, for a fabulous beach vacation with great friends.

Had Stephen been born twenty years earlier, he would not have survived. We were blessed; many prayers from many people were answered. Stephen also did not develop any of the numerous complications associated with his condition.

Today Stephen is twenty-five years old, is 5 feet 9 inches tall, and weighs a healthy 155 pounds. He is a civil-engineering graduate of West Virginia University. Stephen continues to live in West Virginia and is working for a local engineering firm. In addition to being a skilled snow and water skier, he is an accomplished rock climber and scuba diver. I thank God every day for giving us this miracle: the gift of Stephen's life and good health.

Betty Pague

Everyday Miracles

Stephen Pague

Everyday Miracles

STORYTIME FRIENDS

Being a stay-at-home mother with a three-year-old daughter and an eight-month-old son, I was looking for free but meaningful activities to do with my children, specifically, my daughter. We were new to the area and I wasn't familiar with many opportunities. I hadn't met many people yet—particularly people who were home with their children—with whom we could have adventures.

During a visit to the public library, I noticed there was a storytime held once a week for three- to five-year-olds. My daughter loved to listen to stories, and I thought this at last might be an activity she would enjoy. We returned the following week during storytime, and my daughter joined the reading group in the corner of the library, which had a curtain in front of it to section off the area. She was a bit concerned since she didn't know anyone, but I would be waiting close by, running after my son, who was toddling under the library tables.

As I ran after my son, I noticed several of the other parents waiting for their children. There was one mother there who had a young boy in a stroller; he looked to be just a little younger than my son. I thought how nice it would be to get to know someone who had children about the same age as mine. Well, maybe next time I wouldn't be running around as much and I could meet and talk with someone!

Although storytime was supposed to last forty-five minutes, about twenty minutes into the story, two young girls came out from behind the curtain laughing and having a grand time. I took special notice since one of them was my daughter! She and her "new friend," Beth, had been thrown out of storytime because they wouldn't stop talking. The mother I had noticed with the young son in the stroller came over to see what was going on as, alas, Beth was her daughter. We laughed and realized you can't stop a budding friendship. We decided we would have to get these girls together.

This episode started a long-term friendship with the girls, their brothers, their fathers, and their mothers. We had found a gift of a family with whom to explore and have adventures throughout childhood and beyond, and it all began with the everyday miracle of getting thrown out of storytime.

Karen Dickinson

Playtime for the new friends

Everyday Miracles

TAKING ADVANTAGE OF A SECOND CHANCE

During the holiday break in my first year in Temple Medical School, I bumped into a college acquaintance in North Jersey who asked how I was doing. "I'm studying a lot," I said. He replied, "Sounds like you need to get out. Just so happens I'm dating a nurse at Temple who's having a party next Friday; I'm busy, but you should go!"

I tried rounding up some of the usual suspects (classmates) to attend the event, but all were either "booked" or busy. I came home that Friday after a long week and promptly fell asleep.

I woke up about 9:30 p.m. and decided the heck with it; I really did need to get out. Sure, it was late, I didn't know where I was going, and I wouldn't know anyone there, not even the hostess. Being somewhat shy, this was about as bold and uncharacteristic a move as I had ever made. Before I could change my mind, I got in my car and took off.

When I arrived, the party was already winding down. After I met the hostess, Eileen, I wandered around and ended up having a chat with a woman who also didn't know anyone at the party, as she had come with a friend of the hostess. On the way out, Eileen introduced me to a nurse from Temple whom she worked with. "Maybe you'll see her in the hospital sometime," she said.

Next day this shy guy called Eileen for a telephone number. "I don't know Diane, the woman you talked with, she said, "But I can give you

Donna's number; she was the nurse you met on the way out."

Good enough. Wasting no time, I made the call and asked for Diane. "Sorry, wrong number," a sweet female voice replied. Annoyed, I called Eileen to complain about the incorrect number. More annoyed, she pointed out that I HAD SWITCHED THE NAMES, and it was Donna I had called!

Oh well. What the heck. It was a good try.

I immediately called back the same number, got the same sweet voice, and it happened to be Donna's. ... "So, you wanna go out next week?"

Why she agreed to go, I'll never know. I guess maybe because it was just a Tuesday night, not prime time. I got to her place late with maps spread out all over the car, and immediately we had a disagreement about which route I should have taken. (Of course she had lived in the area her whole life and I had just moved to Philly.) Why she agreed to go out *again*, I have no idea. Maybe because I was the first person who ever pronounced her complicated Italian name correctly. Maybe because our first date happened to be on her parents' anniversary.

Or maybe she was just bored and was interested in seeing how far I could go to make a fool out of myself.

To this day, she thinks I was expecting to see her best friend Diane when she opened her door to greet me. I keep telling her, hey, it's easy to confuse *Diane* with *Donna*; I'm just not that good with names.

I don't know why she doesn't believe me. Even after thirty-nine years together.   Jeff Gibson

Everyday Miracles

Donna and Jeff Gibson

TWO WRONGS MAKE A RIGHT

As my family and I left the party held for Mrs. Smith, I thought back to when she and I had first met. I was sorry that I couldn't give my daughter a satisfying answer as to why this once vibrant woman had had a stroke and was confined to a wheelchair.

Looking back. . . .

When I returned to work, my daughter had babysitters who came to the house to watch and care for her. When she turned four, after visiting several schools, I decided to enroll her in a private country day school. It was on one level, clean, and conveniently close to my place of employment, and it had a friendly staff and what seemed like an appropriate curriculum. It was also cheaper than having a babysitter come to the house, and now my child would have other children with whom she could interact on a daily basis. The teachers seemed energetic and creative. Enrolling my daughter in the school appeared to be a good choice: WRONG!

My daughter's class—a combined class of first, second, and third graders—could have had great potential, but for several weeks, the children did little except seatwork on alphabetical order. Yet I had told the teacher that my child could already alphabetize with great skill. I knew that my earlier assumption about the school being right for my child was wrong. It was time for a change.

I enrolled my daughter in the second grade in the local public school. Gone were the before- and after-school programs offered at the private school. I had

Everyday Miracles

to find someone to take care of my child during these times. I inquired at the school and received the names of a couple of women. I visited them and made my choice of a woman whose daughter was also in second grade at the same school. September started and things went well. My decision seemed sound: WRONG! A few weeks into September, the caregiver told me that because of personal issues, she would not be able to continue offering childcare. I was devastated. What was I going to do? I had to work.

I do not recall who told me about Mrs. Smith, but I will be eternally grateful. Mrs. Smith loved children and planned activities for all the kids of varying ages under her watch. The best way to describe the success of her program is to say that when I would leave work at a decent hour and stop at her house to get my daughter, my daughter would frequently hurry to the door and ask if I could come back later to get her. These were not exactly the words a tired, stressed mom wanted to hear, but most times I let my daughter stay.

If the original caregiver had not stopped her babysitting services, my daughter would never have had such a great before- and after-school adventure. I had complete confidence in Mrs. Smith and could concentrate on my job: RIGHT!

So we were very happy to join Mrs. Smith's friends and devoted husband in celebrating her birthday. Many parents there, including my husband, spoke of Mrs. Smith in glowing words. In spite of her debilitating physical problems, as long as she is able to remember her days as a childcare worker, she will stay young at heart.

Madeleine Jones

Madeleine Jones

VINDICATION

There are many great things in life, but few are better than vindication.

I am not talking about being vindictive when the drive to be right overshadows the big picture and hurts others through argumentative, insulting, and hurtful behavior. I am talking vindication, the feeling deep in your soul when personal integrity, honor, respect, and dignity outweigh pettiness, greed, ignorance, short sightedness, and spite toward others.

For instance, who was more vindicated than Noah? He faithfully built the ark and followed God's commands despite the taunting of his neighbors. And let's not forget the Little Red Hen. You best believe she felt vindicated dining on her hot toasty bread after politely telling her farm mates a thing or two about their callous behavior to her.

The story I want to share happened in January 2013, when I left my job after thirteen years for a new opportunity. On my last day, I sat at my computer feverishly finishing a fifty-plus-page strategy document . . . and no one cared. It was not due. My boss had not asked for it. My salary or performance rating did not depend on it.

This project came from what I had seen as a need in our business six months prior and, much to my dismay, became a lonely labor of love. I partnered with a great agency, and no one—neither my boss, his boss, nor the Insights senior leader—could see the value in the work.

Though the funding got cut, I personally had to finish the project, and I put all the knowledge from my head into the strategy document. My soul needed me to complete what I had such passion to do for my own well-being.

I e-mailed the document to my boss, who genuinely seemed baffled that I had showed up, let alone worked until the bitter end. I left the building for the last time feeling very proud of completing something personally important to me.

I assumed it would stay on the company share drive and collect figurative dust.

More than two years later, a friend from my old team told me a product born from my strategy had launched. What? I was shocked. Having anything see the light of day is huge. She said she never forgot my work and used it continuously, including rehiring the original agency to develop the product.

When I heard the news, I told my mother this had to be one of the best moments in my career. Despite the shortsighted, dismissive attitude and malaise from the senior leaders at the time, I felt incredibly vindicated that my vision and work had meaning and worth.

I will not receive accolades, a raise, or a bump in my bonus because of the launch. Most people won't know the role I played in the project, and frankly, it doesn't matter.

What is important to me is that my personal integrity and convictions matter.

Lauren M. Scott

Everyday Miracles

Lauren M. Scott

WHAT HAPPENS WHEN GOD INTERVENES?

One instance when God intervened began in the eighth-grade classroom in Maple Avenue School, in Penns Grove, New Jersey, in 1955.

I sat there at the desk looking at the two choices on the paper. I had to mark one or the other. My heart was in turmoil because the check mark would settle the course of my life for many years. Should I choose *Academic*, which would lead to college, or *Commercial*, leading to a secretarial or clerical position? It was not that I did not know what I wanted. I had great interest in being a teacher or a lawyer (or totally unrelated, an airline stewardess).

The debate team was very exciting and I was good at it. Mother used to say while correcting me, "Harriet, you would make a good lawyer." As the eldest child, I was "teach" when we played school . . . as many times as I could convince the rest to let me.

My dilemma: how could I pay for my education? My dad was a great auto mechanic and a steady worker. He provided for Mother, seven children, a cat, a dog, and a bird. He repaired lawnmowers, grew a huge garden for our food, and sold veggies and strawberries "in town" plus raised chickens.

Mother was not a slacker either. She canned the garden produce and was a great seamstress, producing many of our dresses and play clothes. But never had I heard even a hint about a college or a college fund. So I checked the block for the commercial course. Looking back I realized that either I have a huge memory block or college was never mentioned at home. Neither of my parents had graduated high school. In my mind, I was locked into a blue-collar job.

No one came along to encourage me that there were other possibilities. No one knew my thoughts. How could anyone correct them? It was a lack of communication. But human communication was not the only thing lacking. Communication was also lacking from me to God. As an immature believer, I did not think to pray about this or ask God. I say this because after getting out in the world and seeing what was available to a motivated, hardworking, seeking person, I then encouraged my siblings to investigate loans, scholarships, and other funding possibilities.

The checkmark did determine the direction for my work experience. That did not mean my life was miserable. I saw God provide for me in extraordinary ways, but that is another story. My commercial education did not mean that I lost the dream of teaching or that I never had the opportunity.

The Dream: One commercial school teacher and one Bible teacher really reached me in a profound way. They challenged me to be my best with the information they taught. Their teaching was not just the information but how they cared about me, giving the information for my benefit. They put a desire in my heart to be that helpful to someone else.

The Opportunity: "For we are his workmanship, created in Christ Jesus unto good works, which God hath before ordained that we should walk in them"

(Ephesians 2:10, King James Version [KJV]). Little did I know that God had a plan for me to teach.

It seems when people are FAT (Faithful, Available, Teachable), He has work for them. I was very teachable as I devoured scripture. Soon He began fulfilling my desire to tell others about Him.

I actually had a devotional published in *Secret Place*. This scripture seemed to apply to me also: "And I thank Christ Jesus our Lord, who hath enabled me, for that he counted me faithful, putting me into the ministry" (1 Timothy 1:12, KJV). I was asked to help people explore God's word in the Bible for Sunday school classes. I ended up with a model of the Tabernacle and for twenty years took it on the road doing teaching engagements. For the last six or so years, teaching a Bible study at my continuing care retirement community (CCRC) has kept me busy. It was as if First Corinthians 16:9 were happening right here where I live. It reads: "[F]or there is a wide open door for me to ... teach here. So much is happening ..." (The Living Bible).

Interesting is the fact that for these two teaching jobs (the Tabernacle teaching and the CCRC Bible study), I had asked respected teachers to teach. But each of them in essence said, "You do it!" "Who me?" was my response. They were following the Lord's instructions: "And the things that thou hast heard of me among many witnesses, the same commit thou to faithful men, who shall be able to teach others also" (2 Timothy 2:22, KJV).

The Bible tells us to whom much is given, much is required. Preparation for teaching is real work and sometimes hard work. It is time consuming. But there are rewards. One such is having to shout about the Lord (your teaching lesson) for an hour to people because your group is hard of hearing. You ask how that is a reward. Shouting the lesson points fills your heart with joy. The point comes home to you more than to them. Often it is praising the Lord, which definitely gets your endorphins going. God's way is marvelous.

When you teach Bible, your principal is the LORD God. That causes you to take this teaching very seriously, to be humble and concerned that it is done right. But I have learned this scripture is true: "Faithful is he that calleth you, who also will do it" (1 Thessalonians 5:24, KJV). Through prayer and trust, He will inspire you. Over and over I say to Him, "Help me." Over and over He drops ideas into my spirit in the early dawn before my arising or as I go about my day. Over and over the teacher (Harriet) is taught. God is SO good.

Teaching is loving. You love your subject so much you want others to have it to help them. You care for them enough to give them the gift of this knowledge. In the case of a Bible study, you give them the gift of knowing the LORD God Almighty. Sometimes you get loved back for the gift you give. Now that is definitely a reward.

Now you know how a business-educated student becomes a teacher. It is definitely a God thing. You know how He intervened in this case and the happy, fruitful results of His intervention. And now, I am looking for faithful people who will teach others . . . Are you FAT?

Harriet Widlund

Everyday Miracles

Harriet Widlund

WHAT'S IN A NAME?

I had a somewhat common maiden last name, enough so that there was another person with the exact same first and last name at my doctor's office and I often ran into people with the same last name. I wondered what it would be like to not have to be so careful about identifying myself if I had a more unique last name. At least it was easy to pronounce!

I wasn't thinking about my last name when I applied for numerous teaching positions following my graduation from college with a teaching degree. The market was very tight and the search for a job was frustrating. I was lucky to get a few local interviews, but not lucky enough to land a job. I finally applied in a larger radius and got a call for an interview. As I travelled the hour and a half toward the interview, I wondered what had been in my cover letter or resume that had caught the eye of the principal enough to call me.

The interview was very interesting, as the principal asked nothing about my teaching but was more interested in my plans and getting to know me as a person. During the course of our talk, he asked about my children. As a childless, twenty-one-year-old, new college graduate, the question took me aback. I responded that I didn't have any children yet, but hoped to in the future. With confusion in his voice, he questioned why I had written in my cover letter that after staying home with my children for several years I was looking forward to getting back into the classroom. When he showed me the cover letter he was looking at, I could tell it wasn't mine and told him so. The cover letter was indeed from someone with the exact same name as mine. My blessed name had landed me the interview, and my first job!

Karen Dickinson

(l-r) Johnny, Karen, John, and Jenny Dickinson

Everyday Miracles

WITH A LITTLE BIT OF LUCK

The year was 1979. My family and I were living in North Brunswick, New Jersey, not far from the National Office of the Boy Scouts of America (BSA). I had worked for the BSA for twenty-eight years, and the last twenty of those years had been at their National Office. Then, in a surprise announcement, it was revealed that the BSA would soon move its National Office to the Dallas, Texas, area.

For me, mental turmoil took over. My job was secure, but moving to Texas right then was a problem. I liked life in the Northeast. I was very comfortable in my home and neighborhood. My wife was teaching at Rutgers U. in the middle of working for her doctoral degree. Our son was in Philadelphia preparing to become a physician, and our daughter was at Rutgers on her way to an education career. I was not happy about moving to Big D!

Most of my friends were also not happy, but they thought they "had to go." I also had concerns, the biggest being my ability to find new employment. I was fifty-two years old and had worked for one employer all of my life. However, despite my age and background, I decided not to move.

The move was scheduled to occur in about three months. For the few persons deciding not to move, the BSA offered a short course in job finding and a half-year of pay if you stayed to the last day and helped close the entire office, which employed about 500 people. I said "Yes" and "Thanks" to both offers.

Most of my work at the BSA had been in the areas of writing, editing, internal communications, and public relations. As such, I belonged to several organizations specializing in the public-relations and communications field.

At the next meeting of one of these groups, a fellow member asked me about the move and my plans. Several days after our conversation, he phoned me and said he had just heard about a job in New York City that might interest me and he had told them about me.

I thanked him and set up an appointment at the Manhattan home office of the Public Relations Society of America (PRSA). The thought of commuting to NYC didn't bother me since I knew the city pretty well and many of my neighbors also had jobs in the city. Things went well in the interview, and several days later I got a call offering me the job. "Wow," I thought. I accepted! My prayers had been answered. So, I stayed at the BSA, helped close the office on a Thursday, and began a new job with the PRSA the following Monday. How lucky can you get!!

Unfortunately, the PRSA job was not the greatest. Now comes the amazing part. About eight months into the job, I happened to meet the same fellow who had helped me at another communications group meeting in Manhattan. He told me that he had heard that things weren't going too well at PRSA, and he asked me what I thought. I told him that I was disappointed, but it was a job. He smiled and said he had just heard that the Leukemia Society of America (LSA) headquarters was looking for another PR-type employee and I might fit the bill. So, the next day I had lunch with the big boss at LSA, and a new job!

Who said New York was a tough town? I was lucky... twice. I stayed with LSA for the rest of my career days, retiring twelve years later. I'm happy I didn't go to Texas. I liked New York, liked my job, didn't mind the commute, and had a good life.

Fortunately, I also had a good guardian angel friend... and a little luck!

Tom Gibson

Tom in his office

LOOKING AHEAD

To encourage you to recognize your Everyday Miracles, here are a few memory starters:

- IN MY CHILDHOOD, I . . .
- MY BEST FRIEND
- MY FAVORITE SUBJECT IN SCHOOL
- MY FAVORITE TEACHER
- MY FAVORITE ACTIVITY AS A TEENAGER
- A DREAM THAT CAME TRUE
- A JOB I HELD
- MY SPOUSE
- MY CHILDREN
- MY PARENTS
- A FAMILY PET
- A CHALLENGE THAT TURNED INTO A BLESSING
- A TRIP TO REMEMBER
- AN ENCOUNTER WITH A STRANGER
- A SEEMINGLY MIRACULOUS OCCURRENCE
- AN EXPERIENCE WITH NATURE
- HOW I LEARNED AN IMPORTANT LESSON ABOUT MYSELF

Everyday Miracles

Everyday Miracles

1st row: Jenny Lane, Donna Gibson, Jeff Gibson, Karen Dickinson, John Dickinson; 2nd row: Jeff Lane, Brad Gibson, Greg Gibson, John Thomas Dickinson; 3rd row: Tom Gibson, Margaret Gibson.

And here is the newest generation:

Brady Scott Lane   **Chase Austin Lane**

Everyday Miracles

Made in the USA
Middletown, DE
28 January 2016